D1246878

Armin Haab   Alex Stocker

Lettera 1

A standard book of fine lettering

Standardbuch guter Gebrauchsschriften

Nouveau répertoire d'alphabets originaux

Arthur Niggli Teufen AR

Every purchaser of LETTERA 1 is entitled to form words or texts for any purpose from the alphabets it contains.

The reproduction of newly designed or old but fully revised and/or supplemented alphabets in technical journals, technical books and so forth, whether for purposes of criticism or as illustrative material, is permitted for not more than 8 letters per alphabet and with express reference to the source.

Alphabets of LETTERA 1 which have been newly designed, or old alphabets which have been completely revised and/or supplemented, as indicated in the Index with ©, may be used in technical journals and books and in the printing trade by type founders, photocomposers, decal letter makers, stencil makers, etc. only with the special written consent of the designers. This applies both to the use of the alphabet as such or in the guise of any form of words containing the letters of the alphabet.

Inquiries are to be addressed to Armin J. Haab, Via Collina 43, 6612 Ascona, Switzerland.

Unauthorized use of the alphabets as described above, whether in the form of reproduction or by the printing trade, will be the subject of legal proceedings.

Jeder Käufer von LETTERA 1 hat das Recht, Worte oder Texte für irgendwelche Zwecke aus den vorliegenden Alphabeten zu gestalten.

Reproduktionen von neu entworfenen oder alten, aber völlig überarbeiteten und/oder ergänzten Alphabeten in Fachzeitschriften, Fachbüchern und dergleichen, sei es zum Zwecke der Rezension oder als Abbildungsmaterial, sind nur für acht Buchstaben pro Alphabet mit ausdrücklicher Quellenangabe gestattet.

Alphabete von LETTERA 1, die neu entworfen wurden, oder alte Alphabete, die völlig überarbeitet und/oder ergänzt wurden, wie im Index angegeben mit ©, bedürfen für die Verwendung in Fachzeitschriften und Fachbüchern, sowie durch das grafische Gewerbe wie Giessereien, Lichtsetzereien, Abziehschriftenfabrikanten, Schablonenfabrikanten usw. der besonderen, schriftlichen Genehmigung der entsprechenden Entwerfer. Dies gilt sowohl für die Verwendung des reinen Alphabetes als auch in verdeckter Art, in Form von Worten, die wiederum das Alphabet ergeben.

Anfragen sind zu richten an Armin J. Haab, Via Collina 43, 6612 Ascona, Schweiz.

Die missbräuchliche Verwendung der Alphabete wie oben zitiert, sei es durch Reproduktionen, sei es durch die Verwendung durch das grafische Gewerbe, wird rechtlich geahndet.

Chaque acquéreur de LETTERA 1 a le droit de faire usage des alphabets que nous présentons pour composer des mots ou des textes, ceci dans n'importe quel but.

La reproduction, dans des revues et manuels professionnels, d'alphabets nouvellement créés ou d'alphabets anciens entièrement remaniés et/ou complétés n'est autorisée que pour 8 lettres de l'alphabet en indiquant clairement la source, qu'il s'agisse d'une critique ou d'une matière d'illustration.

L'emploi de nouveaux alphabets de LETTERA 1 ou d'anciens alphabets entièrement remaniés et/ou complétés, comme indiqués dans l'index avec ©, dans des revues et manuels professionnels, ainsi que par les ateliers graphiques, comme des fonderies de caractères, des ateliers de photocomposition, des fabricants de décalques et de chablons, etc., nécessite l'accord écrit des créateurs. Cela est valable autant pour l'emploi intégral de l'alphabet que pour un usage dissimulé sous forme de mots permettant de reconstituer l'alphabet.

Les demandes sont à adresser à Armin J. Haab, Via Collina 43, 6612 Ascona, Suisse.

L'emploi abusif des alphabets, comme mentionné ci-dessus, que ce soit par la reproduction ou par les arts graphiques, sera poursuivi par la loi.

Cada comprador de LETTERA 1 tiene el derecho de crear para cualquier fin palabras o textos sirviéndose de los abecedarios de este libro.

En las reproducciones de los abecedarios de nueva creación o de los antiguos totalmente renovados y/o completados, en revistas y libros especializados y similares, tanto si ello obedece a fines de recensión como de ilustración, sólo están permitidas 8 letras por abecedario y haciendo constar expresamente su procedencia.

Se requiere un permiso especial escrito de los propios diseñadores para utilizar los abecedarios de nueva creación o los antiguos totalmente renovados y/o completados, según están indicados en el Indice con ©, en revistas y libros especializados o a través de industrias gráficas, como fundiciones, fotocomposiciones, fabricantes de letras adhesivas o plantillas, etc., lo cual tiene vigencia tanto para los abecedarios propiamente dichos como para los que, en forma de palabras, dan también una versión encubierta del abecedario.

Para peticiones escribir a: Armin J. Haab, Via Collina 43, 6612 Ascona, Suiza.

La utilización fraudulenta de los abecedarios según se ac mencionar, tanto mediante reproducciones como a través industrias gráficas, será sancionada por la Ley.

© World Copyright 1954
8th, revised edition 1972
by Arthur Niggli Ltd., CH - 9052 Niederteufen, Switzerland
Jacket design by Alex Stocker
Typography and Layout by Armin Haab/Walter Hættenschweiler
Blocks: Neue Chemigraphie AG, Zürich
Printed and bound in Switzerland
by Buchdruckerei R.Weber AG, Heiden AR
Library of Congress Catalogue Card Number 60-50012
ISBN 3 7212 0038 1

in memoriam Alex Stocker

Dear LETTERA Friend,

Taken all round, books on lettering are either a collection of type designs of a predominantly classical pattern or a hotch-potch of a graphic designer's highly personal creations which, properly used, remain his inalienable property. It all depends on who compiled the book.

What the modern designer needs is a book containing both classical and modern types carefully selected for form, originality and utility, and it is precisely this need we have attempted to satisfy with a collection that concentrates on the best faces in everyday use. In making our selection we have been guided mainly by the visual effect of the individual type and have avoided designs unsuitable as display faces because they are of a literary character or too deliberately modish to have lasting worth. In this way we have been able to discard a lot of the padding which usually makes works of this kind so bulky and in return have acquired extra space for some original variations on classical faces and certain rediscoveries from last century in the belief that new forms can help to give variety to the typographic scene.

We begin with ROMAN CAPITALS — the fountainhead of our European printing tradition — show some later derivative forms and then proceed to the BLACK LETTER group. This is limited to five BLACK LETTER ALPHABETS since this face is not fashionable at present and is in any case little favoured in Latin and Anglo-Saxon countries. The series compendiously subsumed under the name ROMAN begins with some delightful Medieval Lettering. The great diversity of this group is exemplified by a miscellany of fancy types of a HISTORICIST persuasion and some original designs — a total of 23 alphabets (five of which were specially drawn for this book) and twice as many word specimens — and by 4 SCRIPT ALPHABETS. To provide good examples of SLAB SERIF the 6 existing alphabets were supplemented by 8 new alphabets upon which the changes are rung in a number of imaginative variations. — Six of the most attractive ENGLISH-ITALIAN alphabets (5 had to be redrawn) and a number of individual characters round off the richly detailed picture of ROMAN types. — After two established and five revised SANS SERIF ALPHABETS together with a colourful variety of word variations we come to the more fanciful creations, the majority of which have not been published before, being produced specially for this book. — This brings to a close the selection of 62 alphabets and more than 190 word specimens from the typeface arsenals of Europe and America, supplemented and completed by examples of our own work. An index gives the character and origin of each individual face.

The abundance of examples, the clarity of the layout and the handy format have already made this book the indispensable vademecum of the modern designer. In more than 70 countries, from Tokyo to Santiago de Chile, from Moscow to San Francisco, the BOOK OF LETTERING has been constantly in use since 1954, a fact which speaks for itself. This 8th edition is being printed on art paper to give a sharper definition for photostat copying and photographic reproduction.

In 1961 the series was continued with LETTERA 2 and in 1968 by LETTERA 3. LETTERA 4, for which considerable preliminary work has already been done, will appear on the market in 1972 and will reflect the latest trends in lettering at that time.

The status of a STANDARD BOOK OF LETTERING now attained by the LETTERAS is due in no small measure to the enormous amount of work — 2000 to 3000 hours per volume — devoted to these books, to say nothing of the expense. Obviously no one but ourselves feels inclined to take up a task of such Sisyphean proportions.

For the production of the typefaces I should like to express my most cordial thanks to the following type foundries: Bauersche Giesserei, Frankfurt/Main; Deberny & Peignot, Paris; Joh. Enschedé en Zonen, Haarlem; Fonderie Typographique Française, Paris; Haas'sche Schriftgiesserei, Münchenstein; H. C. Hypius, Zurich; Stephenson, Blake & Co., Sheffield.

Yours sincerely,

Baar, June 1968

4

Lieber LETTERA-Freund

Schriftbücher sind im allgemeinen, je nach der Tätigkeit Ihrer Hersteller, entweder eine Sammlung typographischer Druckschriften vorab klassischer Schnitte oder ein Sammelsurium eigenwilliger Schöpfungen eines Graphikers, die, richtig angewendet, das Privileg ihres Schöpfers zu sein pflegen. — Was dem Schriftverbraucher unserer Zeit fehlt, ist eine Zusammenstellung jener Schriften, die sowohl die klassischen wie auch modernen Typen kritisch nach Form, Originalität und Brauchbarkeit ausgewählt enthält. Diesem Bedürfnis haben wir mit dieser Sammlung, die sich auf die besten Gebrauchsschriften konzentriert, zu entsprechen versucht. Unsere Auswahl, die vor allem nach der optischen Wirkung der einzelnen Typen vorgenommen wurde, schliesst alle jene Schöpfungen aus, die entweder ihres literarischen Charakters wegen als Auszeichnungsschriften nicht in Frage kommen oder, zu modisch entworfen, wenig Beständigkeit verraten. Damit verzichtet das Buch auf den Ballast, der ähnliche Werke unhandlich zu machen pflegt. Dafür haben wir originellen Spielformen klassischer Schrifttypen und wiederentdeckten Schöpfungen des vergangenen Jahrhunderts um so mehr Platz eingeräumt, in der Annahme, dass neue Formen das Bild der Schrift unserer Tage variieren helfen.
Unsere Folge beginnt mit der Mutter der europäischen Schrifttradition, der ROEMISCHEN KAPITALE, gefolgt von einigen Beispielen ihrer Entwicklungsformen und leitet dann über zur Gruppe der FRAKTUR-SCHRIFTEN. Diese zurzeit wenig aktuelle Schriftform, zudem in lateinischen und angelsächsischen Ländern spärlich gefragt, zeigen wir lediglich in 5 FRAKTUR-ALPHABETEN. Besonders schöne MEDIEVAL-SCHRIFTEN eröffnen die vielfältige Reihe der eigentlichen ANTIQUA. Verschiedenste Zierformen des HISTORISMUS und eigene Schöpfungen — insgesamt 23 Alphabete (wovon 5 eigens für dieses Buch gezeichnet) und doppelt so viele Wortschriften —, ferner 4 SCHREIBSCHRIFT-ALPHABETE beleuchten die mannigfaltigen Abwandlungen der eigentlichen ANTIQUA. — Um die EGYPTIENNE in einwandfreien Vorlagen zeigen zu können, mussten zu 6 bestehenden 8 neue Alphabete entworfen werden, die wiederum in vielen Schriftvariationen phantasiereich abgewandelt sind. — 6 der schönsten ITALIENNE-ALPHABETE (5 mussten neu gezeichnet werden) und zahlreiche Einzelschriften runden das reiche Bild der ANTIQUA-FAMILIE ab. — Zwei bewährte und fünf neu durchgearbeitete GROTESK-ALPHABETE begleitet von einer bunten Fülle von Wortvariationen, leiten über zu mehr phantastischen Schöpfungen, die grösstenteils unveröffentlicht, besonders für dieses Buch angefertigt wurden. — Damit schliesst die Auswahl von 62 Alphabeten und über 190 Wortbeispielen aus den Schrift-Arsenalen Europas und Amerikas, ergänzt und vervollständigt mit Beispielen eigenen Schaffens. — Als Abschluss gibt ein Register Charakter und Herkunft jeder einzelnen Schrift bekannt.
Durch die Fülle der Beispiele, klare Gestaltung und handliches Format ist das Buch bereits zum unentbehrlichen Gerät des heutigen Schriftenverbrauchers geworden. Es wird von Tokio bis Santiago de Chile, von Moskau bis San Francisco, in über 70 Ländern als DAS SCHRIFTENBUCH unentwegt

seit 1954 verwendet, eine Tatsache, die für sich selbst spricht. Zudem drucken wir die 8. Auflage auf Kunstdruckpapier, um durch ein schärferes Bild photokopieren und Photoreproduktion zu erleichtern.
In der Folge erschienen 1961 als Fortsetzung dieses Programms LETTERA 2, und 1968 LETTERA 3, LETTERA 4, für das wir bereits erhebliche Vorarbeit geleistet haben, dürfte 1972 auf dem Buchmarkt erscheinen, und wird die dannzumal allerneuesten Schrifttendenzen aufzeigen.
Dass die LETTERAS tatsächlich zu STANDARDBUECHERN MODERNER GEBRAUCHSSCHRIFTEN geworden sind, ist nicht zuletzt der enormen Arbeit zuzuschreiben, die ein einzelnes Buch verlangt. Liegt doch die Arbeitszeit allein pro Band bei 2000—3000 Stunden, von den Unkosten ganz zu schweigen. Eine solche Sisyphusarbeit nimmt offenbar niemand auf sich, ausser wir.

Für die Herstellung von Schriftsätzen möchte ich folgenden Schriftgiessereien meinen besondern Dank aussprechen: Bauersche Giesserei, Frankfurt/Main; Deberny & Peignot, Paris; Joh. Enschedé en Zonen, Haarlem; Fonderie Typographique Française, Paris; Haas'sche Schriftgiesserei, Münchenstein; H. C. Hypius, Zürich; Stephenson, Blake & Co., Sheffield.

Mit freundlichen Grüssen

[Unterschrift]

Baar, im Juni 1968

5

Cher ami de LETTERA,

Les recueils de caractères sont le plus souvent, selon la nature des travaux professionnels de leur auteur, soit une collection de caractères d'imprimerie de types plutôt classiques, soit une revue des créations d'un graphiste dont l'heureuse mise en œuvre reste le privilège de l'inventeur. Mais ce qui, de nos jours, manque à tous ceux dont le métier exige l'emploi de lettres imprimées ou dessinées, c'est une collection des diverses écritures réunissant les caractères tant classiques que modernes, soigneusement sélectionnés d'après leur forme, leur particularité et leur utilité pratique. C'est cette lacune qu'entend combler le présent recueil, soucieux de répondre à un désir généralisé.

Notre choix obéit principalement aux critères de l'effet visuel des divers caractères; il exclut toutes les créations d'une mode trop éphémère ou d'une forme littéraire qui ne s'adapte guère à la mise en évidence des mots. L'ouvrage renonce de ce fait au leste superflu qui rend certains ouvrages analogues peu maniables. En revanche, nous avons accordé d'autant plus de place à des créations du siècle passé, redécouvertes, en admettant que ces formes anciennes contribuent à varier l'image de l'écriture contemporaine.

Notre recueil commence par la CAPITALE ROMAINE, mère de toute la tradition des caractères européens, suivie de quelques-unes de ses diverses formes historiques, avant d'arriver au groupe des CARACTERES GOTHIQUES. Nous n'en publions d'ailleurs que cinq alphabets, le gothique étant de nos jours peu usité et rarement demandé dans les pays latins ou anglo-saxons. De très beaux exemples médiévaux introduisent l'abondante série des CARACTERES LATINS. Les formes ornementales les plus spécifiques de l'Historisme ainsi que des créations personnelles — vingt-cinq alphabets (dont cinq dessinés exclusivement pour ce volume), une cinquantaine d'ensembles composés et quatre ALPHABETS D'ANGLAISE dérivés du romain — illustrent les multiples métamorphoses des caractères latins. Afin de présenter dignement l'EGYPTIENNE, il nous a fallu, à six alphabets existants, en adjoindre huit nouveaux spécialement dessinés à cet effet et se prêtant, eux aussi, à de nombreuses variantes d'une heureuse recherche. Enfin, un choix restreint à six des plus beaux ALPHABETS D'ITALIENNE (cinq durent être dessinés à nouveau), ainsi que divers exemples autonomes complètent cette revue de la grande et célèbre famille du ROMAIN. Sept LINEALES, dont deux préexistantes et cinq nouvellement élaborées, accompagnées d'une suite de variations, présentées sous forme de mots, préludent à des créations d'ordre plus fantaisiste, pour la plupart inédites et spécialement conçues pour la présente publication. Ainsi s'achève notre choix groupant soixante-deux alphabets, de près de deux cents exemples de mots empruntés aux trésors des caractères d'Europe et d'Amérique, plus un certain nombre d'exemples de nos propres créations. Un index signale l'origine et la nature de cette moisson de caractères.

Par la richesse de ses exemples, par la clarté de sa disposition intérieure et le choix de son format d'une manipulation aisée, ce livre est devenu un outil précieux, indispensable à l'utilisateur de caractères d'imprimerie contemporains. Il est utilisé depuis 1954, en tant que Nouveau répertoire d'alphabets originaux, dans plus de soixante-dix pays, de Tokyo à Santiago du Chili, de Moscou à San Francisco. Nous imprimons cette huitième édition sur papier couché afin de faciliter la reproduction photographique et d'assurer un œil plus net. Nous avons fait paraître LETTERA 2 en 1961 et LETTERA 3 en 1968. LETTERA 4, pour lequel nous avons élaboré déjà de gros travaux de préparation, sera probablement édité en 1972 et contiendra les tendances les plus nouvelles dans le dessin des caractères.

Le fait que les ouvrages LETTERA soient devenus des RECUEILS STANDARDS DE LETTRES ET CARACTERES MODERNES est dû au travail méritoire consacré à la réalisation de ces volumes, soit 2000 à 3000 heures pour chacun d'eux, et ce sans parler des frais. Un tel effort est certes peu commun.

Pour les compositions typographiques figurant en ces pages, je me fais un plaisir d'exprimer ma gratitude particulière aux fonderies: Bauersche Giesserei, Francfort-sur-le-Main; Deberny et Peignot, Paris; Joh. Enschedé en Zonen, Haarlem; Fonderie Typographique Française, Hypius, Zurich; Stephenson, Blake & Co. Ltd., Sheffield.

Avec nos sentiments amicaux

Baar, juin 1968

6

A B C D

I J K L M

Q S T U

E F G H

N O P R

W X Y Z

COLUMNA

ABCDE

FGHIJKLM

NOPQ

RSTUVW

XYZ

IMPERATOR

DOUBS

ZVG

LA TIERRA
DE
DON VASCO

ARKADIA

valais

LA SEMANA SANTA DE SEVILLA

A B C D E

F G H I K L M

N O P Q R S T

U V W X Y Z

a b c d e f g h i j k l m n

o p q r s t u v w x y z

L O N D O N

Cölnisch Current

Fette Gotisch

A B C D E F G H I
K L M N O P Q R S
T U V W X Y Z

abcdefghijklmnopqr
stuvwxyzchck
&fiflßtz

Joh. Sebastian Bach

Fraktur

A B

R L M N O

V W X Y Z

l n o p q r s s t u v w x

ff fi fl ll ſi ſl ſt ß tz

Fette Altfraktur

A B C D E F G H I
K L M N O P Q R
S T U V W X Y Z

abcdefghijklmnopq
rſstuvwxyzchckffffflfl&ſſſiſtßz
1234567890

Christian Morgenstern

Uppenzell

17

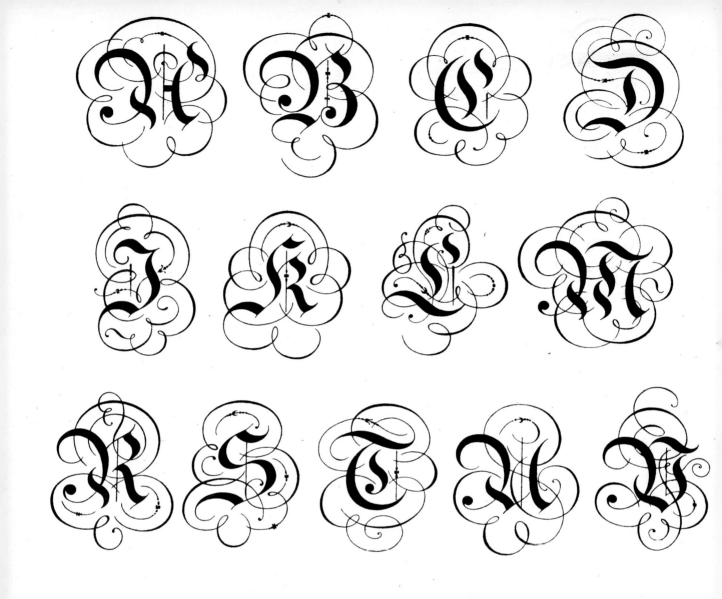

abcdefghijklmn

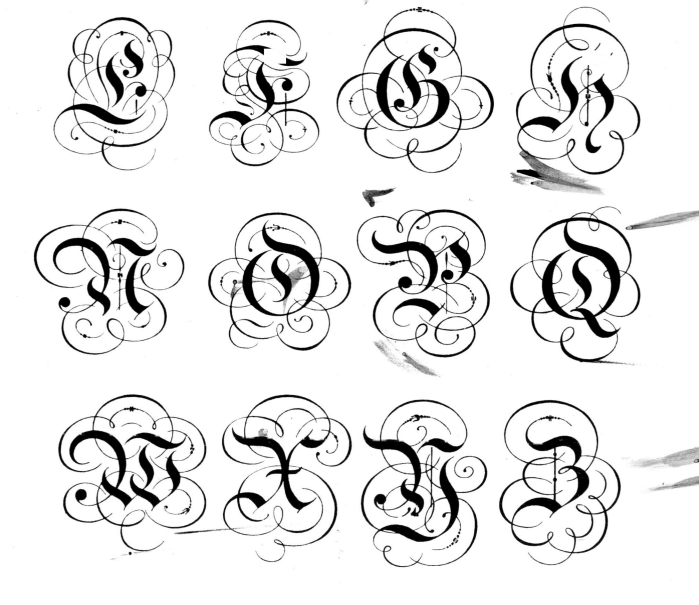

opqrſstuvwxyz

19

Garamont romain

ABCDEFGHIJKLMNOP
QRSTUVWXYZ
abcdefghijklmnopqrstu
12345 vwxyz 67890

Garamont italique

ABCDEFGHIJKLMNO
PQRSTUVWXYZ
abcdefghijklmnopqrstuv
12345 wxyz 67890

ABDGM&NPRTV

l'après midi d'un faune

A B C D E

F G H I K

J L M N O

P Q R S T

U W X Y Z

A B C D E

F G H I K

L M N O P

Q R S T V

X Y Y Z

Caslon's Roman

ABCDEFGHIJK
LMNOPQRST
UVWXYZ

abcdefghijklmnopqr
stuvwxyz
1234567890&

SHAKESPEARE

Caslon's Italic

A B C D E F G H I J K L
M N O P Q R S T U
V W X Y Z

*A B C D E G F K M N P
Q R U T Y*

a b c d e f g h i j k l m n o p q r s t u
v w x y z h k v v w æ œ fl ß ch ck &
1 2 3 4 5 6 7 8 9 0

ELIZABETH

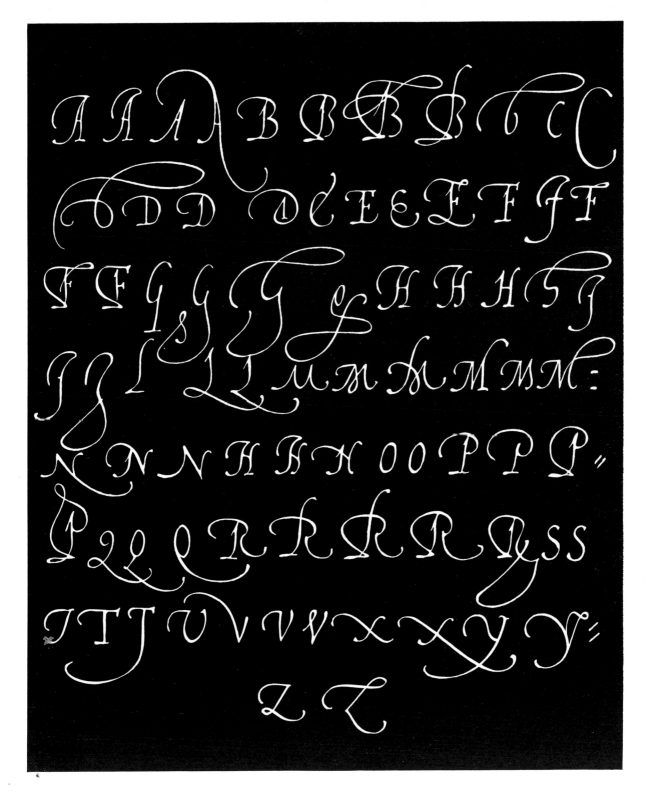

The original dies of
this famous historic
design known as
Baskerville Old Face
were engraved
about 1768
abcdefghijklmnopqrst
uvwxyz
12345&67890

ABCDEF

GHIJKLM

NOPQ

RSTUVW

XYZ

H.MOORE

Bodoni-Antiqua

ABCDEFGHIJKLMNOP
QRSTUVWXYZ
abcdefghijklmnopqrstu
12345 vwxyz 67890

Bodoni-Kursiv

ABCDEFGHIJKLMNO
PQRSTUVWXYZ
abcdefghijklmnopqrstu
12345 vwvwxyz 67890

A B C D E

F G H I J K

L M N O P Q

R S T U V

W X Y Z

A B C D E F

G H I J K L

a b c d e f g h i j k l m n o p q

r s t u v w x y z N

½ 1 2 3 4 5 6 7 8 9 0 ¾

O P Q R S T

U V W X Y Z

32

ABCD
EFGHIJK
LMNO
PQRSTU
VWXYZ

123
4567890

LATIN

ABCDEFG
HIJKLMNO
PQRSTUV
WXYZ

1
234567890

LA
CIUDAD
DE
MEJICO

Mannequin

ABCDEFGHIJKL
MNOPQRSTUV
WXYZ

abcdefghijklmnopqr
sutvwxyz

1234567890

CIRQUE

A B C D E F

G H I J K L M

N O P Q R S T

U V W X Y Z

ANGLAISE

B C D F G H I J

abcdefghiklmnop

K L M N O P Q

qrstuvwxyzzäöü&

R T U V W X Y Z

1 2 3 4 5 6 7 8 9 0

Antoine de Saint-Exupéry

MINDEN

NURNBERG

ABCDEFGHIKLM

ROBINSON

QRSTUVWXYZ

MISSION

ABCDEFGHI
JKLMNOPQRST
UVWXYZÆŒ

abcdefghijklm
nopqrstuvwxyz

1234567890

Ombres
et lumières
Les
jeunes filles
en
fleurs

ABCD
EFGHI
JKLMN
OPQR
STUVW
XYZ

ABCDEFG

HIJKLM

NOPQRST

UVWXYZ

FLORES

EISEN

CONGONHAS
DO
CAMPO

U P R E T O

Throwsosl's

ABCDEFGH
IJKLMN
OPQRSTUV
WXYZ

abcdefghijklmn
opqrstuvwxyz

FAT ITALIC

MAMA

Auction

GINEVRA

JOCRISSE

AMEN

SMART

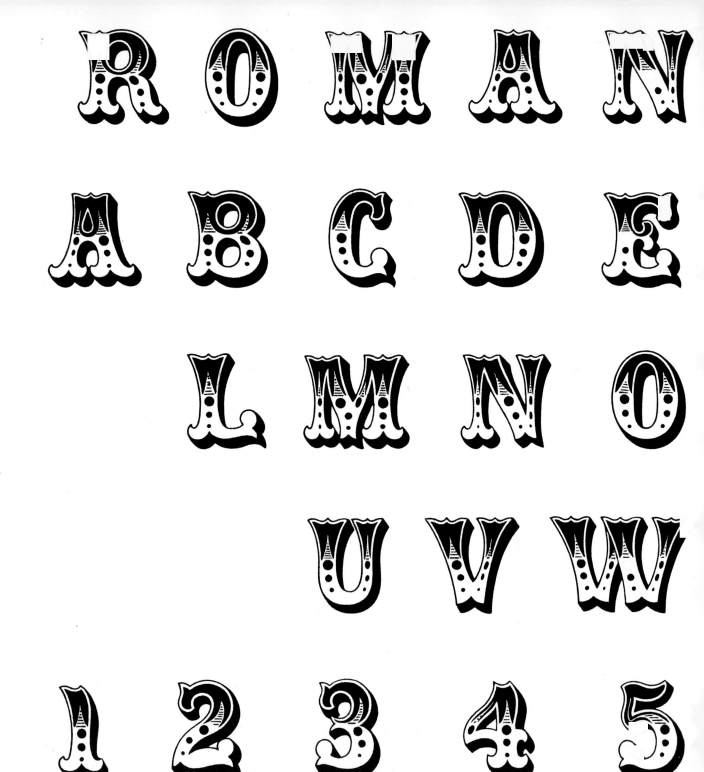

ABCDEFGHIJ
KLMNOPQRS
TUVWXYZ

abcdefghijklm
nopqrstuvwxyz

1234 5&67890

50

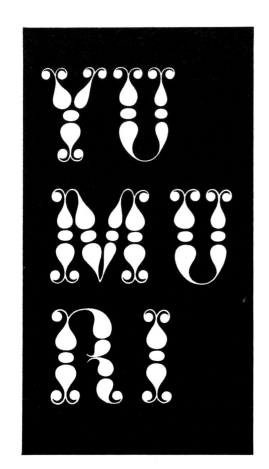

MORELIA

FLORIDA

ITALIA

COTILLION

RIO PAPALOAPAN

TRADITIONS

BINGEN

COPA CABANA

HISTORIA

MEDIEN

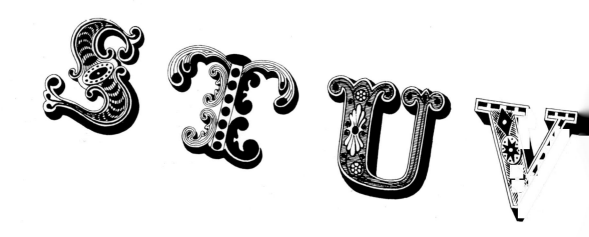

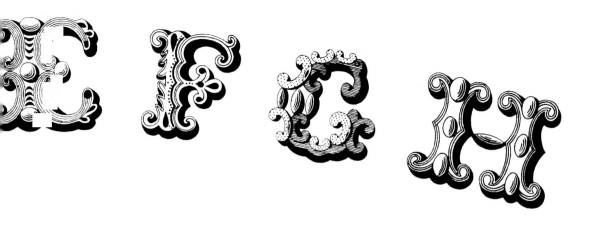

CHISEL

Aa Bb Cc Dd Ee

Ff Gg Hh Ii Jj Kk

Ll Mm Nn Oo Pp

Qq Rr Ss Tt Uu

Vv Ww Xx Yy Zz

1 2 3 4 5 6 7 8 9 0

URI

LAS
TE
HUA
NAS

UTAH

BAHIA

Clarendon

ABCDEFGHIJ
KLMNOPQRST
UVWXYZ

abcdefghijklmno
pqrstuvwxyz&ßfi
1234567890

CHURCHILL

AIR MAIL

A B C D E F G H
I J K L M N O P
Q R S T U V W
X Y Z

TAL DER KŒNIGE

LA
JEUNESSE
DOREE
DE
BAAR
LES
BAINS

PROFIL

A B C D E F G
H I J K L M N
O P Q R S T U
V W X Y Z

1 2 3 4 5 6 7 8 9

BRAQUE

A a   B b   C c

H h   G g   I i

M m   N n   P p

T t   U u   W w

D d   E e   F f

J j   K k   L l

Q q   R r   S s

X x   Y y   Z z

DANGER

ABCDEF

GHIJKLMN

OPQRSTU

VWXYZ

MEXICO

KOPINIA

NEON

PUEBLA

SAVOIR BOIRE

varios aspectos

JUAN GRIS

abcdefghij
klmnopqrs
tuvwxyz
1234567890

ABCDE
FGHIJKL
MNOPQ
RSTUVW
YZX

FOREST

ABCDEFG
HIJKL
MNOPQRS
TUVWXYZ
HOUSE

INDIEN

MONNEROD

COLORADO

BOOTIA-PHOKIS

JOHNSON

ARIZONA

LA CONQUISTA

A B C D

E F G H I J K L M

N O P Q R

S T U V W X Y Z

1 2 & 3 4

5 6 7 8 9 0

INITIALES

COMPACTES

ÉCLAIRÉES

RED

ABCDEF

GHIJKL

MNOPQR

STUVW

XYZ

ROSES

ABCDEF

GHIJK

LMNOP

QRSTU

VWXYZ

RODIN

LESLIE

CALDER

SYMPHONIE

DISNEY

CARON

KLEE

PAULISTA

ERNST

THE
GOLDEN

PUEBLO

DOCUMENTS

EAST
TO
WEST

DIABLE

ABCDEFG

HIJKLMN

OPQRSTU

VWXYZ

ABCDE
FGHIJK
LMNO
PQRSTU
VWXYZ
ÆŒ

CUBA

. . . .

A B C D
E F G H I
J K L M N
O P Q R
S T U V W
X Y Z

FONDERIE

KEINE SONNE

PAPANTLA

HEINRICH

LOS ANGELES

MONTE CASSINO

THE NEW BOOK

LA FIESTA DE MARIA CANDELARIA

      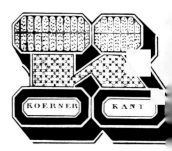

DAGUESSEAU.

ESMENARD.

FLORIAN.FOY

GOETHE

L.AHARPE.LEIBNITZ

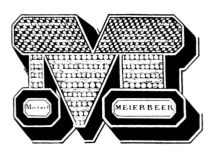

Mozart   MEIERBEER

PERRAULT

QUINAULT

RABELAIS   Rossini

SCHILLER.SAUL.

YOUNG.YRIARTE

Z.SCHOKKE.ZEA

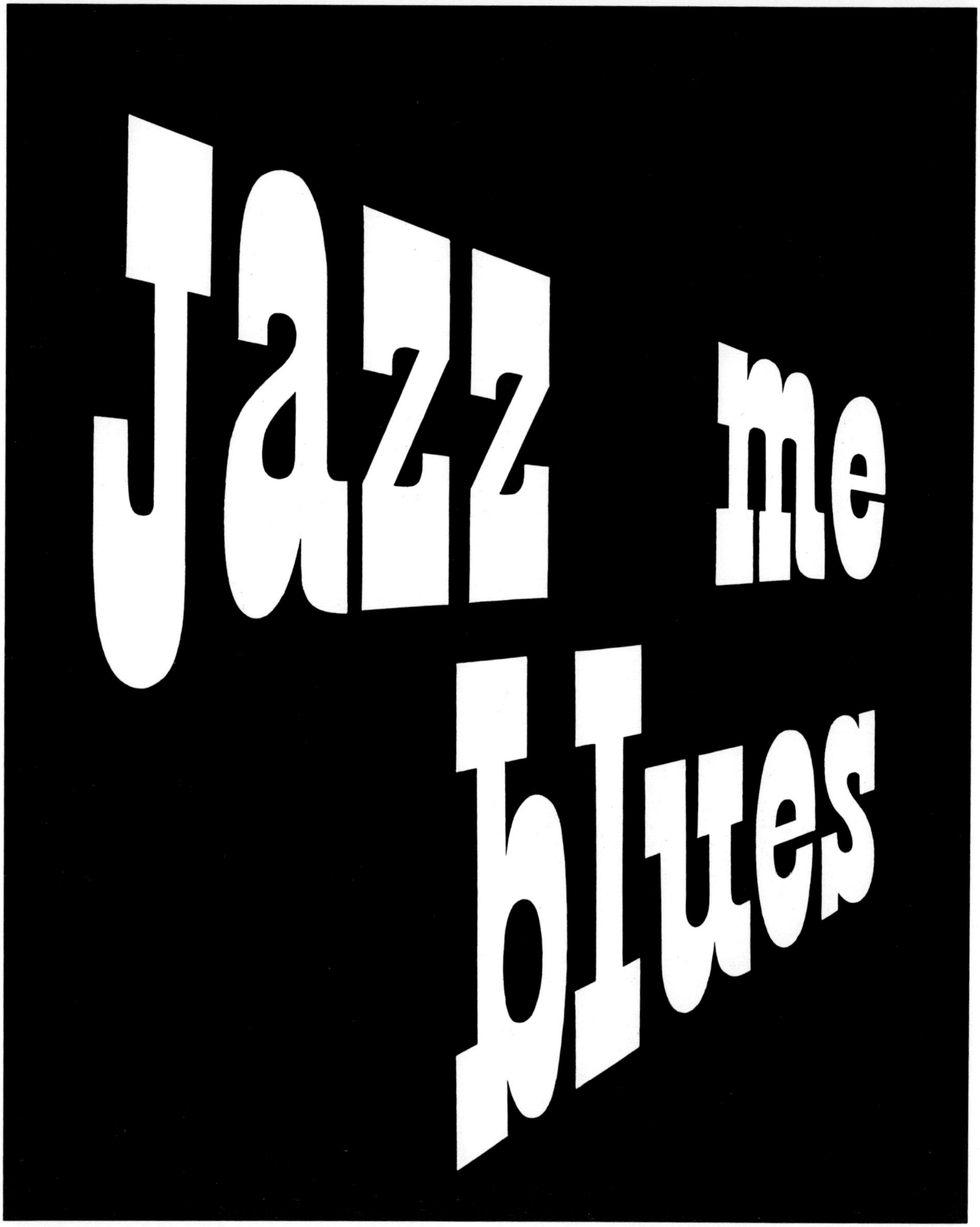
Jazz
me
blues

Italienne

A B C D E F G H I J
K L M N O P Q R S T
U V W X Y Z

a b c d e f g h i j k l m n o p q
r t s y v w x u z

1 2 3 4 5 6 7 8 9 0

KID ORY

ABCDEFG
HIJKLM
NOPQ
RSTUVW
XYZ

RENE CLAIR

Jazz at the Philharmonic

VOGUE

A B C D E F G

H I J K L M N

O P Q R S T U

V W X Y Z

CABARET

CASINO

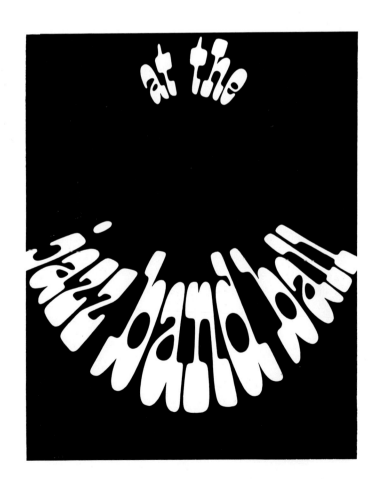

INITIALES

A B C D
E F G H I J K
L M N O P
Q R S T U V
W X Y Z

ECLAIREES

En
los
Jardines
de
España

OTHELLA
STROZIER

SAN
FRANCISCO

H·O·M·E

ESPAÑA

CHIRICO

ORNEMENTS

DANZANTES

BENSHEIM

CHIAPAS

JUANITA

ABCDEF

GHIJKLMN

OPQRSTUV

WXYZ

HOME

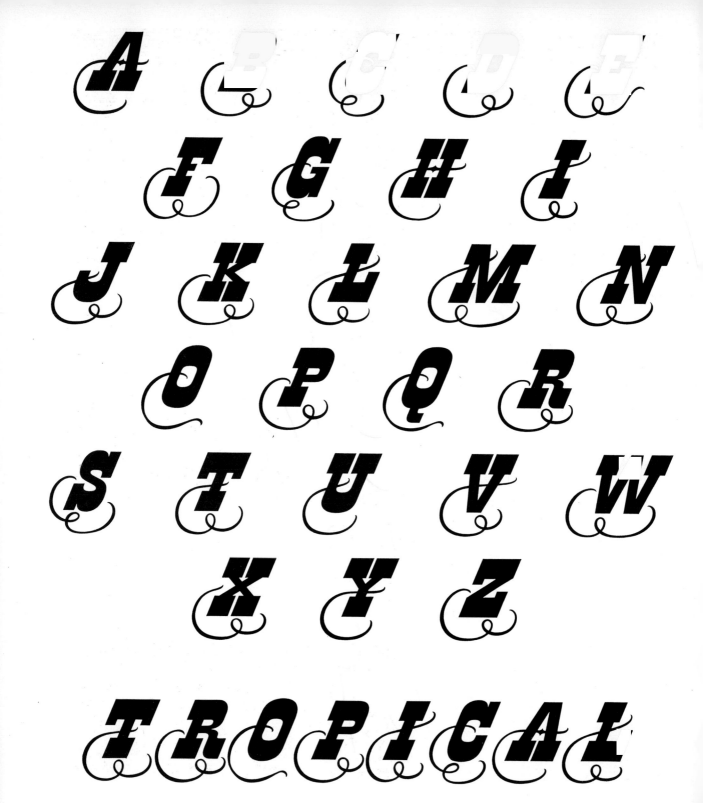

Akzidenz-Grotesk

ABCDEFGHIJKL
MNOPQRSTUV
WXYZ

abcdefghijklmnop
qrstuvwxyz

1234567890?!&

GAMBRINUS

ABCDE

FGHIJKLMN

OPQRSTUV

WXYZ

Commercial-Grotesk

A B C D E F G H I J
K L M N O P Q R S T
U V W X Y Z

abcdefghijklmnopqrst
12345 uvwxyz 67890

OSCAR NIEMEYER

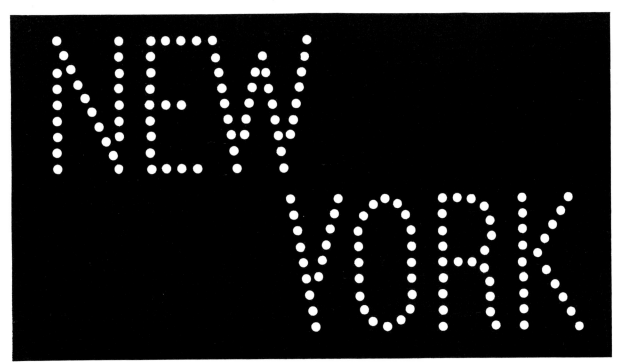

MEXICO

JOHN

OLYMPIA

PARICUTIN

ATHEN

PATRAS

OAXACA

PICASSO

mondrian

BAUHAUS

marino marini

CONGO

ABCDEFG
HIJKLMN
OPQR
STUV
WXYZ
abcdefghik
lmnopqrstu
vwxyz
12345
6789!

ABCDEFGHIJK
LMNOP
QRSTUVWXY
Z
1234567890

NEW YORK

ATTIKA

GRAPHIQUE

new york

MIDDLE WEST

SÃO PAULO

TYPINE

RHYTHM
KINGS

XOCHI
CALCO

belo horizonte

LIENIS

UR
SCHWEIZ

BACFDE
GHJKLM
NOPRTS
UYIXWZ!

abcdegh
imjknlopq
rfswtxyz

ZUERICH

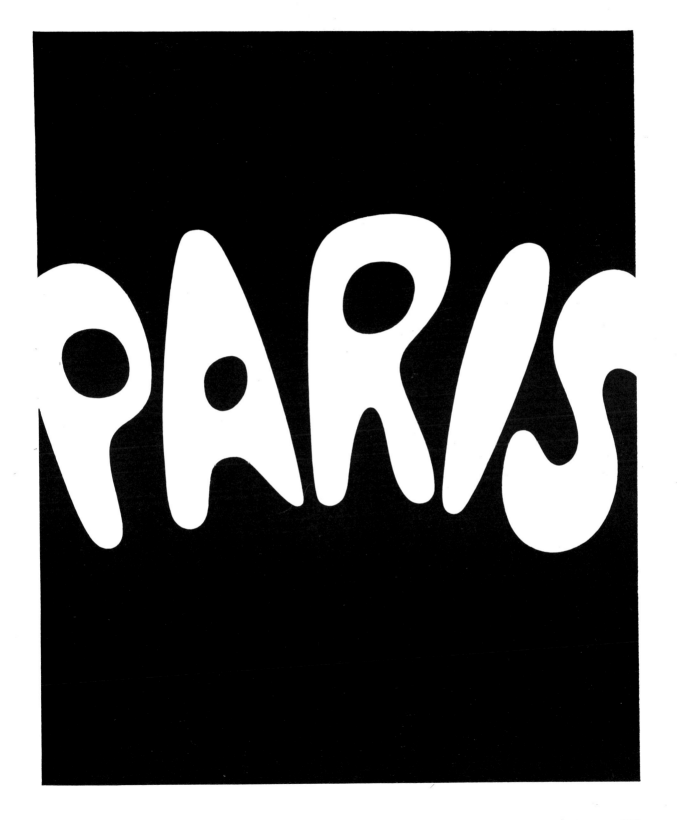

ABCDE
FGHIJK
LMNOP
SROTUV
XVWZI

schenk
ein
buch

AZTEC

TENOCHTITLAN

KARNAK

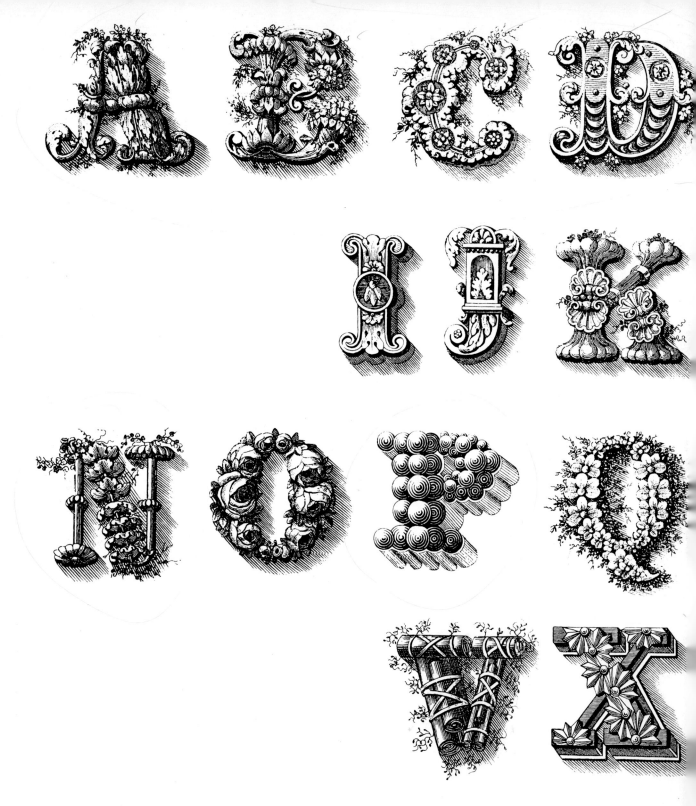

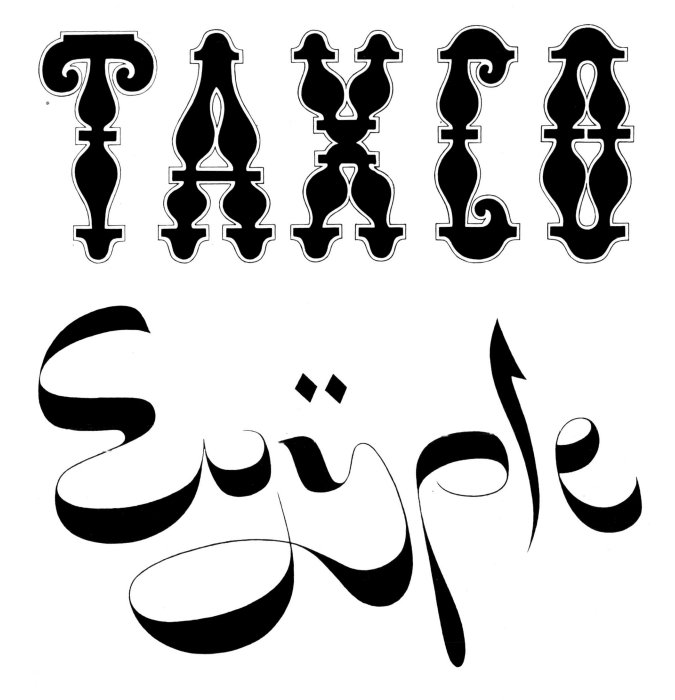

TAXCO

Egypte

JOHN J. ASTOR

TLACO
TLAPAN

OAXACA
DE
JUAREZ

TEOTIHUACAN

SALVADUR

foto

BAHIA

DALI

audrey hepburn

INSPIRE

Jerry Mulligan

CITY LIGHTS

Der blaue Engel

Index

Abbreviations / Abkürzungen / Abréviations / Abreviaturas

D: Designed by: / Entworfen von: / Dessiné par: / Diseñado por:

RC: Redesigned and completed: / Völlig überarbeitet und ergänzt: / Redessiné et complété: / Diseñado de nuevo y completado:

TF: Type-foundry: / Schriftgiesserei: / Fonderie: / Fundición tipográfica:

FP: From the printers: / Aus der Druckerei: / De l'imprimerie: / De la imprenta:

©: World-Copyright by / ©: Welt-Copyright von / ©: Copyright mondial par / ©: Copyright mundial de

†: Not available (only used when a type foundry or a printing office is mentioned)

Nicht lieferbar (nur angegeben, wenn eine Giesserei oder eine Druckerei miterwähnt wird)

Hors commerce (n'est indiqué que dans les cas où une fonderie de caractère ou une imprimerie sont également mentionées)

Fuera de venta sólo se indican cuando se mencionan al mismo tiempo una fundición tipográfica o una imprenta)

Date following the character's or designer's name indicates approximate year of creation

Jahreszahlen einem Schrift- oder Künstlernamen folgend geben das ungefähre Herstellungsjahr bekannt

La date qui suit le nom du caractère ou du dessinateur indique approximativement l'année de la création

Le fecha que sigue a los nombres del carácter o del diseñador indica aproximadamente el año de creación

Page / Seite / Página

8—9 ROMAN CAPITAL (1954); RC: Alex Stocker, Baar; ©: Armin Haab

10 COLUMNA (1953); D: Max Caflisch, Bern; TF + ©: Bauersche Giesserei, Frankfurt/Main

11 DOUBS; ZUG; LA TIERRA...; ARKADIA; VALAIS; LA SEMANA... (1954); D: Alex Stocker; ©: Armin Haab

12 GROOTE CANON DUYTS (1748); D: Joan Michael Fleischmann; TF + ©: Joh. Enschedé en Zonen, Haarlem

13 FETTE GOTISCH (1860); TF + ©: Haas'sche Schriftgiesserei, Münchenstein BL

14—15 CÖLNISCH CURRENT FRAKTUR (1590) †; TF: D. Stempel AG, Frankfurt/Main

16 FETTE ALTFRAKTUR (1840); TF + ©: Haas'sche Schriftgiesserei, Münchenstein BL

17 A; APPENZELL (1954); D: Alex Stocker; ©: Armin Haab

18—19 KANZLEISCHRIFT (1889); D: Ludwig Petzendorfer, Stuttgart; RC + ©: Armin Haab

20 GARAMONT ROMAIN / ITALIQUE (1530); D: Robert Granjon; TF + ©: Deberny Peignot, Paris

21 L'APRES-MIDI...; D: Alex Stocker; ©: Armin Haab

22 ROSART GESCHADUWDE KAPITALEN (1743); D: J. F. Rosart; TF + ©: Joh. Enschedé en Zonen, Haarlem

23 ROMAN ALPHABET (1523); D: Ludovico Vicentino, Venezia; RC + ©: Armin Haab

24 CASLON'S ROMAN (1716—28); D: C. William Caslon; TF + ©: Haas'sche Schriftgiesserei, Münchenstein BL

25 CASLON'S ITALIC (1716—28); D: C. William Caslon; TF + ©: Haas'sche Schriftgiesserei, Münchenstein BL

26 REDONDILLA (1570); D: Francisco Lucas, Madrid; RC + ©: Armin Haab

27 BASTARDA (1577); D: Francisco Lucas, Madrid; RC + ©: Armin Haab

28—29 BASKERVILLE OLD FACE (1782 ?); D: Isaac Moore; TF + ©: Stephenson, Blake & Co., Sheffield

30 BODONI-ANTIQUA / KURSIV (1818); D: G. B. Bodoni, Parma; TF + ©: Bauersche Schriftgiesserei, Frankfurt/Main

31 DIDOT; D: Firmin Didot (1764—1836); TF + ©: Deberny Peignot, Paris

32 IDEAL SCHREIBSCHRIFT; TF + ©: D. Stempel AG, Frankfurt/Main

33 MODERN ART (1954); D: Alex Stocker; ©: Armin Haab

34 INITIALES LATINES BLANCHES A FILETS; TF: Deberny Peignot, Paris

35 LA CIUDAD...; D: Alex Stocker; ©: Armin Haab

36 MANNEQUIN (1954); D: Alex Stocker / Hans Gruber, Zürich; ©: Armin Haab

37 THE BLUES; NEW ORLEANS; D: Alex Stocker; ©: Armin Haab

38 ANGLAISE †; FP: Unionsdruckerei, Bern; RC + ©: Armin Haab

39 CIRQUE (1954); D: Alex Stocker, ©: Armin Haab

40 MINDEN †; NURNBERG †; ROBINSON †; MISSION †; TF: Haas'sche Schriftgiesserei, Münchenstein BL; AB—M; Q R—Z; RC + ©: Armin Haab

41 GRAS SERRES ITALIQUE (1840); D: Laurent, Deberny; TF + ©: Deberny Peignot, Paris

42 OMBRES ET . . .; D: Alex Stocker, ©: Armin Haab

43 MACDONALD (1820–30); RC + ©: Armin Haab

44 FLORES (1954); D: Alex Stocker / Hans Gruber, Zürich, ©: Armin Haab

45 EISEN †; TF: Haas'sche Schriftgiesserei, Münchenstein BL; GONGONHAS DO . . .; UPRETO; D: Alex Stocker, ©: Armin Haab

46 THOROWGOOD'S FAT ITALIC (1820); D: Robert Thorne; TF + ©: Stephenson Blake & Co., Sheffield

47 MAMA; GINEVRA; D: Englisch; AUCTION †, SMART † (1821); TF: Vincent Figgins, London †; JOCRISSE; D: Alex Stocker, ©: Armin Haab; AMEN (1834) †; FP: Johnson & Smith, Philadelphia †

48–49 ROMANTIQUE; TF: Fonderie Typographique Française, Champigny

50 CHAILLOT (Typophanes); D: Marcel Jacno; TF + ©: Deberny Peignot, Paris

51 YUMURI, MORELLA, FLORIDA, RIO PAPALOAPAN; D: Alex Stocker, ©: Armin Haab; ITALIA; D + ©: Armin Haab: COTILLON †; TRADITIONS †; TF: Haas'sche Schriftgiesserei, Münchenstein BL

52 BINGEN †; HISTORIA †; MEDIEN †; TF: Haas'sche Schriftgiesserei, Münchenstein BL; COPACABANA; D: Alex Stocker, ©: Armin Haab

53 OLIVIA (1954); D: Alex Stocker, ©: Armin Haab

54–55 ALPHABET FANTASQUE; RC + ©: Armin Haab

56 CHISEL (1850); TF + ©: Stephenson Blake & Co., Sheffield

57 URI; UTAH; LAS TEHUANAS; MITLA; BAHIA; D: Alex Stocker, ©: Armin Haab

58 CLARENDON; D + ©: Haas'sche Schriftgiesserei, Münchenstein BL

59 FOTO; D: Alex Stocker, ©: Armin Haab

60 AIR MAIL (1954); D: Alex Stocker, ©: Armin Haab

61 TAL DER . . .; D: Alex Stocker, ©: Armin Haab

62 La JEUNESSE . . .; D: Alex Stocker, ©: Armin Haab

63 PROFIL (1943); D: Eugen + Max Lenz, Zürich; TF + ©: Haas'sche Schriftgiesserei, Münchenstein BL

64–65 EGYPTIENNE (1954); D: Alex Stocker, ©: Armin Haab

66 DANGER; D + ©: Paul Sollberger, Bern

67 MEXICO; KOPINIA; NEON; PUEBLA; VARIAS ASPECTOS; D: Alex Stocker, ©: Armin Haab; SAVOIR BOIRE; D + ©: Walter Herdeg, Zürich

68–69 JUAN GRIS (1954); D: Alex Stocker, ©: Armin Haab

70 FOREST HOUSE; D + ©: Paul Sollberger, Bern

71 INDIEN †; MONNERAD †; JOHNSON †; TF: Haas'-sche Schriftgiesserei, Münchenstein BL; COLORADO; BOEOTIA-PHOKIS; ARIZONA; LA CONQUISTA; D: Alex Stocker, ©: Armin Haab

72 INITIALES COMPACTES ECLAIREES; TF + ©: Deberny Peignot, Paris

73 RED ROSES; D + ©: Paul Sollberger, Bern

74 INITIALES OMBREES; TF + ©: Deberny Peignot, Paris

75 LESLIE; CALDER; DISNEY; CARON; KLEE; D + ©: Walter Hættenschweiler, Zug; SYMPHONIE; RC + ©: Armin Haab

76 PAULISTA; ERNST; THE GOLDEN; A; PUEBLO; DOCUMENTS; EAST TO WEST; D: Alex Stocker, ©: Armin Haab

77 DIABLE; D + ©: Paul Sollberger, Bern

78 OMBREES ORNEES (1820); D: J. Gillé; TF: Fotosatz Morografic, Merkurstrasse 35, 8032 Zürich

79 CUBA (1954); D: Alex Stocker, ©: Armin Haab

80 FONDERIE †; KEINE SONNE †; HEINRICH †; MONTE CASSINO †; THE NEW BOOK †; TF: Haas'sche Schriftgiesserei, Münchenstein BL; PAPANTLA; LOS ANGELES; D: Alex Stocker, ©: Armin Haab

81 LA FIESTA . . .; D: Alex Stocker, ©: Armin Haab

82–83 ALPHABET LAPIDAIRE MONSTRE (1834–35); D: Jean Midolle; RC + ©: Armin Haab

84 JAZZ ME BLUES; D: Alex Stocker, ©: Armin Haab

85 ITALIENNE (1954); D: Alex Stocker / Hans Gruber, ©: Armin Haab

86 KID ORY (1954); D: Alex Stocker, ©: Armin Haab

87 FOTO; RENE CLAIR; JAZZ AT . . .; D: Alex Stocker, ©: Armin Haab

88 VOGUE (1954); D: Alex Stocker, ©: Armin Haab

89 DURZUG; D + ©: Eugen Hotz, Baar

90 ZENTRALE; D + ©: Eugen Hotz, Baar; HOT; BOUTIQUE FANTASQUE; FOTO; AT THE JAZZ . . .; D: Alex Stocker, ©: Armin Haab

91 CHIRICO; DANZANTES; CHIAPAS; D: Alex Stocker, ©: Armin Haab; ORNEMENTS †; BENSHEIM †; TF: Haas'sche Schriftgiesserei, Münchenstein BL

92 JUANITA (1954); D: Alex Stocker, ©: Armin Haab

93 HOME SWEET HOME; D: Alex Stocker, ©: Armin Haab

94 TROPICAL (1954); D: Alex Stocker, ©: Armin Haab

95 EN LOS JARDINES . . .; OTHELLA STROZIER; SAN FRANCISCO; HOME; ESPAÑA; D: Alex Stocker, ©: Armin Haab

Page / Seite / Página

96   INITIALES ECLAIREES; FP: C. J. Bucher, Luzern

97   SEVILLA; D: Alex Stocker, ©: Armin Haab

98   HALBFETTE AKZIDENZ-GROTESK; TF + ©: H. Berthold AG, Wien; FP: A. Hürlimann, Zürich

99   GAMBRINUS; D + ©: Paul Sollberger, Bern

100   HALBFETTE COMMERCIAL-GROTESK; TF + ©: Haas'sche Schriftgiesserei, Münchenstein BL

101   NEW YORK; STOP; D + ©: Armin Haab

102   MEXICO; OLYMPIA; PARICUTIN; ATHEN; PATRAS; OAXACA; D: Alex Stocker, ©: Armin Haab; JOHN; FP: Bruce, David & George, New York †

103   PICASSO; MONDRIAN; BAUHAUS; MARINO MARINI; CONGO; D + ©: Walter Hættenschweiler

104   BREITFETTE GROTESK (1954); D: Alex Stocker / Hans Gruber, Zürich, ©: Armin Haab

105   SCHMALFETTE GROTESK (1954); D + ©: Walter Hættenschweiler

106   NEW YORK; ATTIKA; NEW YORK; MIDDLE WEST; TYPINS; SAO PAULO; D: Alex Stocker, ©: Armin Haab; GRAPHIQUE; D: H. Eidenbenz, Basel; TF + ©: Haas'sche Schriftgiesserei, Münchenstein BL

107   RHYTHM KINGS; XOCHICALCO; BELO HORIZONTE; LIENIS; URSCHWEIZ; D: Alex Stocker, ©: Armin Haab; INDIAN COUNTY; D + ©: Armin Haab; HAAS †; TF: Haas'sche Schriftgiesserei, Münchenstein BL

108   ZÜRICH (1954); D: Alex Stocker / Hans Gruber, ©: Armin Haab

109   PARIS; D: Alex Stocker, ©: Armin Haab

Page / Seite / Página

110   GROTESK (1954); D + ©: Walter Hættenschweiler

111   SCHENK EIN BUCH; D + ©: Walter Hættenschweiler

112   QP-U; PARODIES; RC/D: Alex Stocker, ©: Armin Haab

113   ASSUAN; TENOCHTITLAN; KARNAK; D: Alex Stocker, ©: Armin Haab

114—115 ALPHABET (1841); D: Fratelli Santerini, Cesena / Raffaele Radisini, Bologna; RC + ©: Armin Haab

116   CHLAUSJAGEN; D: Alex Stocker, ©: Armin Haab

117   TAXCO; EGYPTE; D: Alex Stocker, ©: Armin Haab; JOHN J. ASTOR †; FP: Bruce, David & George, New York †

118   TLACOTALPAN; OAXACA DE JUAREZ; TEOTIHUACAN; D: Alex Stocker, ©: Armin Haab

119   SALVADOR; FOTO; BAHIA; D: Alex Stocker, ©: Armin Haab

120   EBONY; PANAMA; D: Alex Stocker, ©: Armin Haab

121   DALI; D + ©: Armin Haab; AUDREY HEPBURN; D + ©: Walter Hættenschweiler; INSPIRE; D + ©: Otto Glaser, Lugano

122   INTERIOR; D: Alex Stocker, ©: Armin Haab; COCTEAU; D + ©: Walter Hættenschweiler

123   LÜGE UND ZAUBEREI; D: Alex Stocker, ©: Armin Haab

124   JERRY MULLIGAN; CITY LIGHTS; DER BLAUE ENGEL; D: Alex Stocker, ©: Armin Haab

125   D'ALTRI; MARCEAU; LA REGLE DU JEU; D: Alex Stocker, ©: Armin Haab

833   494